AF444084

WHO ME? YES, YOU!

MAKING CHANGES

SCOTT ROTH

Scott Roth
Who me? Yes, you!: Making Changes

All rights reserved
Copyright © 2023 by **Scott Roth**

No part of this publication may be reproduced, distributed, or transmitted in any form
or by any means, including photocopying, recording, or other electronic or mechanical
methods, without the prior written permission of the publisher, except in the case of
brief quotations embodied in critical reviews and certain other noncommercial uses
permitted by copyright law.

Published by BooxAi
ISBN: 978-965-578-694-1

1

IGNITING THE SPARK: WHERE CHANGE GETS A FIRESTARTER

I AM amazed at how tragic events can sear our memories and replay vividly.

I walked out my front door and saw the neighbor girl sitting *criss-crossing applesauce* in a circle where the sidewalk met the driveway of their home. She was weeping with a group of friends. The news of their friend taking his life was spreading quickly. His choice, driven by a lack of will to live, would send ripples through time and space. We are never prepared to hear such news. Never...

Watching them weep affected me deeply. It shook me to my core. The following days unfolded, leading up to a funeral. I was asked to be an on-site grief counselor for the students. The service was held at a nearby local church. The family of the deceased were people of faith. Even with their faith, this was a tragic time. The need for a larger church became apparent. This particular church was chosen because of its capacity to accommodate a large number of people. The impact was greater than I had anticipated.

The family selected a pristine white casket. The purpose was to allow students to process their grief by writing notes on the casket using permanent markers. This practice was something I had never witnessed before. In my profession as a pastor, I have been a part of many funerals over the years, but this was a new experience for me. As I sat in the entranceway, I observed student after student writing notes on the casket. Quotes of encouragement, terms of endearment, and Bible verses were among the things being written.

I remember one student who sat with me; we will call him Jimmy. Jimmy is the typical name I use to keep people anonymous. You may see Jimmy again… but a different Jimmy. Jimmy asks profound questions about life, death, and the reality of being alive without his friend. I continued to talk with various students, consoling them offering encouragement, and praying with them during their grief.

A day or two later, my anger boiled over, and I cried with all my being. I was sitting on the back deck of my townhouse, looking up at the sky, so angry because another life had been taken by suicide. I have been in those spots encouraging students to live. Talking to them in desperation, working through the questions, keeping them calm, and guiding them away from the metaphorical cliff of despair. Now, I wish I could have done something more for this boy. Why, God, couldn't I have stopped it? Could someone have stopped it? The anger grew even more. This boy had faith, a family, and all the reasons to continue living in my mind. Yet it was my perspective.

Then, the thought burned into my brain so profoundly that it seared my memory to this day.

"I have the free will to make a difference... I have a choice."

It was a wrestle with God that day to realize that a human can choose. I needed to take this holy discontent and anger towards suicide and the pain I have witnessed in students and turn it into an empowering energy for change. This was the moment of truth. It was time to rise and find others who were equally outraged at what was happening around us.

All it took was for me to open my mouth. I spoke out to those around me about how I was feeling. During a meeting with a few other pastors, it became evident that I was agitated. I told them that I couldn't handle the mess anymore. Why do we constantly feel stuck when it comes to suicide and, for that matter, all the other problems that plague students? I am just tired of it all. My frustration grew and grew as I spoke.

In that meeting over lunch, a few of us took a stand. We had a reality check and realized that we needed to take a stand.

You may think that you are alone most of the time, but you aren't. It takes a reality check that we need to open our mouths and let it all out. Emotionally vent all the pent-up junk inside of us. I don't mean getting on social media and venting about the issues. No, I mean sincerely expressing our emotions and letting others know that there is a lot of pain in the world. Let out that you are hurting inside because you are watching good people get hurt. Whatever it may be, many times we bottle our emotions and put on a facade. This is what I know: *TELL IT OUT*, don't just keep it inside. Sit with people and express the fact you are hurting. You see, by letting it out people can sit with you, listen, and take action. They may console you, tell you that it's okay, or let you know that many people feel the same way. Sure, it's comforting, but the most important thing is that you are being heard. The best reaction is when someone encourages you to make a change.

That's what happened to me. I was in that room with my colleagues when I realized that I was not alone. We started to dream about what it would look like. Dreaming is a state where you begin to overcome your problems. Dreaming is where solutions happen. So many times, we fail to realize that we have a choice in the matter!

You show ways to solve the problem when you reach a dream state. The dream state is the place where you are making the choices to make things better. The dream state is the spot that takes you to a place where you know it can be done.

Dreaming allows us to create the future. That spot creates a space in time and the reality that we have a potential shot to make all this happen. Sure, dreaming is dreaming. Some dreams are unrealistic. I am talking about dreaming with possibilities. What does the solution to your problem look like? What happens when you sit in a circle, share your pain, and then ask, How do we change this?

We all have choices to make. We can wake up in the morning and be numb to our situation, or we can stand up and choose to change it. Free will is so powerful. We don't have to be alone. At that moment, I sat with my colleagues and realized I was not alone. I also realized we had a chance to make a real difference. It was a reality check within this conversation; we could make a difference.

I remember when I was fat. I was so overweight I was not too fond of it. I would look at myself in the mirror and wonder how I got there. I would wear clothing that hid my fat, and many times, when I looked in the mirror, I kept my body turned just right so that I didn't see how fat I was. It was pretty simple. I was a big dude, and I could wear it well. Or so I thought. I felt good even though I knew I wasn't happy with it. Walking was work, and my ankles were not pleased with me. My doctor would tell me every visit that I needed to slim down and lose some. Over and over, I would hear it and know it.

I never took the time to dream about what it would be like to lose weight. What did it look like on the other side of it all? Instead, I found ways to justify my weight and keep it around. Eating the foods that made me feel good inside rewarded me for who I was because I was fat, and it was okay to eat that stuff because my mind was critical. I hated being fat. I wouldn't say I liked the feelings and all that came with it. My body was meh to me, and it was what housed my mind and soul every day. I decorated this misery the best I could so I didn't have to deal with it. In the end, I had tried repeatedly to lose weight, but I felt hopeless and decided I probably would have to live with it.

I didn't realize how amazing it would be on the other side. At that moment, I had to understand and grab hold of the reality that there was a better life beyond this pit of misery I had put myself in. I had to dream about what it would be like to walk without pain. To move freely and feel healthy. To ride a bike and not have all that weight around me. Just to be free from this burden I put on myself. I had to dream about this unknown joy to start to motivate me to lose weight. That was the reality of it all. I had to start climbing out of my pit and moving to a better place.

Feeling helpless is a perspective that we put on ourselves. Helplessness comes from the fact that we think we can't do it anymore. We create a state of mind to make ourselves feel better. You heard me right. It is something that we do to keep ourselves in the pit of whatever it is that makes us upset. Whatever has you down, putting yourself in a hopeless state gives us a way out. "I don't have to do that because... it's a lost cause". "I am not good enough, so I don't have to solve it." "Being hopeless gives us the right to stay in that space and not do anything about it. In reality, it is a place where we don't have to act.

The hopeless state is something that we, in the end, give ourselves an out for not going on the adventure. I am a big adventure story guy. I love a good story. The heroes of stories do not become heroes because they have a helpless perspective. No, they become the hero because they are overcoming the situation. They are finding the path and moving forward. They are going to chase after the unknown joy that lies ahead. They are redeeming their spaces.

See, hopelessness puts us in a pit. Imagine a pit that is all around you. Walls that keep you from climbing out. This pit you are in can be any subject, but ultimately, it is a pit. As you live in your pit, you begin to decorate it. You hang out there, and you become comfortable. In the pit, it's safe to live and exist. You don't have to deal with it if you don't look at the walls and the pit floor. Right? Out of sight, out of mind. It is an old tactic that humans have been doing for years. We create these facades to help us feel better. We avoid it.

I am getting old and gray, so I am dyeing my hair. I am getting fat, so I wear slimming clothes, primarily black. I am addicted to soda, so I drink diet soda. You can think of many ways to decorate your pit and make yourself feel better. The fact is you are still in the pit. The pit creates a safe place because you know how to deal with it. It is a known misery. Or, as the old saying goes, you deal with the devil, you already know. We can live in denial and be in our misery because we make it comfortable. It's safer than the work to climb out of it to a level of unknown joy. Known misery seems better than unknown joy.

Unknown joy is that state when we are out of the pit. We are still determining what it looks like on the other side. We achieve this space when we are out of the pit. That moment that a person that is abused leaves their abuser. When we start volunteering at a soup kitchen, the state of joy is because we have a burden for people without housing and unsheltered. I don't know if there are so many analogies around unknown joy, but we need to find this for ourselves. We need to dream.

We must come to a place where making the change is very important to all of us. We must take hold of this choice to climb the ladder out of our pit and start moving up and out of where we are. See, the reality check with this is simple. We will always stay in denial, and the issue will always be there unless we take that first step to climb out of the pit. Oh, and remember, there is this cheering section we have behind us. All those people that you have told about your issue are right there. The fact is that you can make a change, and it is right there. The caring people around you are here to love you. They are present to help you climb out. But you have to climb. You make a difference. You are the factor in the equation. You were made for this.

Many times in life, we take for granted what is happening around us. As Edmund Burke said, "The only thing necessary for the triumph of evil is for good men to do nothing." I use this as a mantra when I dream about solving a problem. If I can conceive of a practical and authentic solution, I am actually on the path to making it happen. What happens if I want to avoid seeing a change? When we go back to the example before about suicide and its impact on me. I could discuss it with others and get it on the table. I dreamed of seeing students grow up feeling supported in their lives. There were spaces and people around them caring about them. They had all this available to them. Yet I was the one carrying the dream. I was the one who was holding on to this moment in my mind that the world could be a better place.

I grabbed this, and I was like, "Hey! Wait, I think this can be done." Now I have to ask what happens if I do this. Well, my town would be a better place. It would be a place where we had resources for people in need. For those in pain, we could handle it. There was a space where we could create relationships to support and grow a student. They didn't have to be alone. Yet here I am in my head, dreaming it all up. It was simple. I had to do it. Why did I have to do it?

Because what would happen if I didn't? What did the world look like if I didn't take action? What if I sat back and didn't care? I started to look at that image a bit. It was a short look. Dreaming about me not taking action created another timeline. This timeline is where I didn't take action. I didn't care, and I didn't move forward. The reality is this. It doesn't look good. I see more death. I see pain. I see kids making poor choices. I see families devastated, not by suicide but by kids going down horrible paths in life because they didn't know better. I saw mothers crying and fathers losing their minds because they couldn't do it alone. Yeah, it was pretty messed up looking at what if I didn't take action. Reality is that we can play the what-if game in our mind to a negative or a positive state. All we need to do is focus on the positive state.

Ultimately, when we start to dream, we have to look at both sides of the coin. What if a person like me doesn't take action... and what if I do? I guarantee you that taking action is going to win out. If we keep battling this in our heads over and over this reality, we can make a difference. That we can take a step forward and make a change. There is something about that. This reality check shows that if we can make a difference, we can make a dent in the evil around us. We have the power to make a choice. A choice to do good and set a reality into place that is far better than the other timeline.

I am finding more and more in life that problems keep happening because nobody takes a stand. In our minds, someone else is more qualified and can make this happen. In my life, I roam in different spaces from time to time that I am in over my head. Yet, there is nobody else there to make it happen. I am the expert in areas of things because, well, nobody else is doing it. Think about this for a moment. If you are playing baseball and you are that person who keeps hitting home runs repeatedly. Everyone else around you isn't hitting home runs regularly... you are the expert at it. It's that simple. See, in our world, so many times, we are looking for people to be more qualified because of what they have learned. The fact is you become qualified because of what you have done. Your track record qualifies you. You become someone who knows more than the rest, making you an expert. I know it sounds silly, but this is the reality of life. As you rise and learn and do more, you become better. A much better version of yourself than before.

I remember a time in my life when the Internet was a blazing frontier: Everyone wanted to get ahead and stake their claim. In 2000, people were booming online. It was the wild frontier in cyberspace. I wanted to make a career change when all this was happening. An interview was set up for me through a friend to become a consultant for a company. They wanted to use a new type of technology and advance their product line. All I had to do was prove that I knew more than the company's CEO, and he would hire me. It was hysterical in my mind. I could be an expert in a field by knowing more than this CEO. Well, that's how it happens. I researched and wowed the guy with ideas and thoughts because I was casting a dream. It was that simple. A dream. It was about knowing more than the person in front of me. I was that person taking things to another level, and I did. Why? The CEO cast a dream for a product that he wanted to do and was getting folks around him to make it happen. I was to be one of those people. Why? Because I had the knowledge and ability to apply it... and nobody else did in his sphere of influence.

See, it is about realizing you were made for the moment.

This is a shameless plug for *Young Life*, a fantastic youth organization I am tied to. They have the phrase "You were made for this" to encourage adults to reach out to students. Encouraging adults to know they were made to engage in the youth culture. Good phrase, huh? Always use the phrases you love; it keeps you moving forward!

2

BREAKING THE MOLD:
NAVIGATING THE UNCHARTED

I HAD a situation where a man came into my sphere of influence and unsheltered. It was this awful situation where a perfect storm of lousy stuff culminated in his life, and boom! He was working, sick, and living in his car in January. January in Florida isn't that bad, but January here in Pennsylvania is *cold*. This particular winter, it was cold, chill to the bone cold. When someone has nowhere to live in the winter, we immediately think of heading to a public shelter and getting warm. Right? It is that easy. Go somewhere and get warm. Survive. You can do it. I want you to picture in your mind what that may be like. Putting yourself in a space with a bunch of strangers to sleep in a bed in a room with those strangers. I hope that the night is safe.

We do not understand sometimes that when we have a decision to make, we have to make it. It's so easy for us to ignore that call. Right? I mean, we don't have to deal with it. We can pass it on to the experts. What if there was no expert to pass it on to? If someone has a broken leg in front of me, I know where to go, who to call, or what hospital to drive them to. What if there wasn't a hospital? What if there was no doctor? What if it was me alone and my knowledge of first aid to aid the person with the broken leg? Then, it is up to me to help. So often, we look at situations and play it over and over in our heads why someone else should do it. The fact is we are the ones set to make this happen.

Unsheltered people are an ongoing issue in my suburban rural town. When someone has no place to live, and I find them, there are some things I know to do. I know there are specific numbers to call. When calling, it invokes a process to whisk the person off into the sunset, never to be homeless again. Well, I wish it was that easy. We don't have an excellent clean system like we would if you broke your leg. The fact is that unsheltered in my area means you feel hopeless. There needs to be a clear ladder to climb out of the pit. You break your leg, you go to the hospital. You become unsheltered. You go out and survive on the streets and in the woods. When writing this book, I follow the steps I teach you to solve this issue. There is no hospital for the unsheltered to become not sheltered and thrive in life.

I only know a few others who understand how to get it done when it comes to an unsheltered person. See, I have had experience and engaged the topic for so many years that many call me during a crisis. This is where it gets interesting. Look at yourself for a moment. If you have a heart and a desire to make a change, then you are the perfect person to handle this. When dealing with Jimmy, I had someone come to me, and the conversation went like this:

So, you have this guy you are helping, and why does it have to be you?

I don't know anyone else to help him except me. No, I mean there has to be someone else to handle this.

Nope.

Someone else has to be able to take this issue and handle it.

If you go into your phone and look down at your contacts. Then go to Google and search. Who would you call?

Silence

Exactly.

You.

We are the right person for the job at that moment. Could I find an expert in another town, city, or state? Sure, but in my town, I was the guy to handle this situation and move it forward. So often, we want someone else to address the issues. The reality is that if you are the person having the feelings and the interest, then you are that someone. So many times, many people ignore the issue or want to throw money at it so someone can handle it. The fact of the matter is someone has left. Someone has decided not to do this anymore, and you are it. You are reading this book because someone isn't handling the issue. Time and time again, we, as humans, want to pass the buck. Well, as the line says, the buck stops here. Are you willing to have it stop here? Because this is what I know. I wasn't right away.

I grew up believing I could buy what I needed when I wanted it. As a matter of fact, at an early age, this started with the magic box. You know that magic box in the kitchen we all had growing up? We open the magic box, and food is in there. I never put the food there. I could always get it, but I only did something to get it there. Time and time again, I would go to the magic box and find the food I liked. Then, if it didn't have what I wanted, I told my mom, and magically, the food appeared the following week. The magic box represents how we operate many times in the United States. I see most more developed countries wrestle with this as well. Consumerism is the attitude that we want to consume things to feel better.

Feel safe. There is this reality to how we live: we buy our emotions and our safety. Think about your home and how you live. Let's do this. Take a moment and inventory the room or space you are in right now. What do you see on the walls? What devices are around you? What brands of items do you see? As I write this, I wear two branded shirts that advertise for the companies. I have 4 monitors on my computer and some pretty plush lights that are bumping to the beat of the music. If I went into detail, my room would be a shrine to consumerism.

HAH! It is fascinating when we stop and take inventory of what is happening around us for a moment. The best thing to say to all this is to understand the culture around you and the fact that consumerism has kept you from solving the issue.

Think about all the needs and the problems in our communities, and it comes from the sheer fact that the world revolves around us. Look out your eyes. The world revolves around you. Everywhere you walk, sit, or move, you can spin your head and have this conceptual view that the world is all around you. It is a sheer fact that we feel this way. Then you take this view of the world that revolves around me and couple that with all the emotions and needs of life. We start to build a world-view that it is all about me. Consumerism wants it to be about you. There was a period in the United States when there was only one kind of salt you would buy at the general store. It was the local salt. You came from the local salt mine and went to the store and bought your salt. Now? Go into a grocery store sometime and take note of all the types of salt you can buy now. It's crazy!!! Humans have found a variety of ways to package and sell salt. Why? Because the more varieties we have, the more options we have, making us feel good to have options. We feel empowered in our buying.

Now, take this attitude of buying power and couple it with the desire to see change. I watch so often on social media that if someone shares a post, it's like they are assisting with the cause. We use our influence in small ways to make us feel like we are doing big things. Sure, is it a reality check that there is a false sense of engagement? Sure. Do I love it when someone shares my posts on social media? Absolutely! It all boils down to recognizing that we are in a system built upon us, not having to do a lot but buy a lot. Over and Over, people are looking for something in return. Fundraising has come to a point where people want to buy something, and the profits go to the organization. We must do more than donate our money fully. Instead of just giving a dollar, we need to buy a candy bar. Girl Scout Cookies are a case in point. Sure do. I love them absolutely. Would I give money to the Girl Scouts if they asked for it? Probably not, but do I donate when those Thin

Mints come knocking? YOU BET! I sometimes keep a few boxes in the freezer for the right occasion.

Time and time, over and over, the things of this world do not change because of consumerism. Yet, this goes to a deeper root in our lives. Humans have this direct desire to want what we can't have. We are driven inside of us to move for more. Drew Holcombe has a great song about this: You Want What You Can't Have. In his Lyrics, he states, "You want what you can't have. Since the Garden of Eden, it's been like that." Whether you are a bible person or not. I do want to illustrate this story for you.

Adam and Eve and the Garden is a space where we see this desire for more. God tells Adam and Eve that they can eat anything in the Garden except the fruit from the tree of the knowledge of good and evil. See, this is what cracks me up. Adam and Eve have everything in the Garden. They have a real-life magic box! All the food they can harvest is there. The perfect space, so to speak, to enjoy life. Yet, we see this innate desire to want what we can't have. Why am I going through all this? Look inside yourself. That route of wanting what you can't have may be what drives you more and more in life. You may have to look at this deeper because it is the very thing that has been holding you back from not moving forward with the issues you see around you. The fact is that wanting things takes our time and energy away from caring about others. This stops us from stepping forward and changing because we must focus on enjoying the nicer or finer things.

Don't get me wrong; I am not telling you to buy cheap non-quality items. Not saying that at all. Make sure you check yourself. Take inventory of your motives and how you spend your time. This inventory and looking at yourself will be the main weights that will slow you down in making a difference. In my life, stepping out and solving issues has become a lifestyle. Breaking this habit of making it about me has changed my pace. Now, I want you to understand I am not saying neglect yourself. I know what that looks like.

It is so easy to go too far and burn yourself down. It is easy for us to go fast and race down the line and make things happen and keep trucking week after week and not care about ourselves. There is a balance. If we tip the scales too far and do not make it about ourselves, we will find ourselves in an awful spot. I remember the summer of 2019. It was a time before we ever heard the term COVID. I was living a life that felt very selfless. Week after week, I was engaged with youth, particularly finding at-risk teens. I always always always have this way of drawing in the students on the margins. Looking to build the communities for the students that were hurting. Now, that summer, it was rough. I was fundraising to keep my job as a youth worker for Young Life. Now, let me give you some backstory so you can appreciate this. For most of my adult life, I have been cobbling different jobs together to keep working with at-risk teens. I will be telling you more about this later. But for now, I want you to understand that working for Young Life was my dream job.

Over the years, I worked in many different spaces to volunteer, run my community-based initiatives, and make a difference. Working for Young Life, I felt that I had arrived. I was in my zone and at the right spot. Yet that summer, I was questioning it all. The workload to fundraise was significant. It's more incredible than I ever felt before. I was used to selling my talent and services for money. Now, I just wanted people to give it to me. It was for a good cause, but didn't feel that way. That summer, in particular, life was getting rough. I didn't feel I had a solid community around me; the pressures were closing in. It was that dark day when I was in my basement, and I collapsed in tears, weeping and crying out for a change. The stress was too great on me, and I felt like the world revolving around me was against me and not for me. I was engaging in a systematic approach that needed to be fixed, and I needed to improve. This failing feeling made me fall, and I fell hard. I lay in the basement in a fetal position, crying, and couldn't stop. I knew something had to change, but I didn't know what.

As I write this, I can't express how hopeless I feel. I had some complex issues with students that weren't getting fixed. I felt like I couldn't keep stuff together and was just stuck. I don't even know as I write this. At the same desk and the same chair that, I laid on the floor crying even can be conveyed. I wasn't suicidal, but man, it was close. Close. Okay, so anyway, let's talk about the steps that made me realize my self-care balance was off. Mind you, one extreme is full-blown consumerism. The other side is a mental breakdown. Keep that in mind. It's all about you or not about you at all. This is a danger dangerous space to be in on either side. I say this because I never.

This is because I never had anyone tell me this stuff. It was more to make sure you take care of yourself, but in the end, I didn't know what I was in for.

Okay, so we are either self-centered or losing our minds. So, what is that sweet spot? I went off to *Young Life*'s new staff training for 10 days in the hills of an Oregon Desert. WOW, that was a place. A camp nestled in, well, I say this, a resort in the hills of the Washington Family Ranch. The ranch itself was formerly an occult place that was then busted by the FBI. The property was donated to *Young Life*, and this ranch was now this fantastic oasis in the desert. Funny how things get redeemed. This space became my sanctuary, where I was taught by very selfless people how to have a balance. A balance of mind, body, and soul. A space that showed me how to be in balance. I walked out of there with a new sense of being. I had some spiritual moments along the way that are for another time. I don't want to get too caught up in that; I know I had some "miracles" go on, which also shaped me. I don't want to assume you and I have the same worldview. I want to respect that. Things will often fall into place, and I must acknowledge them somehow because they are outside myself.

There it was; I learned how to sit with myself and have peace. Peace that I was okay. I can't do everything, and I still need to do something. *Young Life* that week, through their staff, taught me this concept of self-care. I heard about it but always thought it meant taking breaks and eating well. I spent the following months on a journey of self-care that has been amazing. It's because I fell in love with caring for myself so I could make a difference in the world around me. This balance of releasing consumerism, not being all about the cause, but how to have a balance about me and the space around me. Part of this balance, too, is understanding myself. In comes Author Ian Crohn. He wrote a book called Road Back to You. It is a powerful book if you have lost your way in self-care. He is an expert on the mystical art of the Enneagram (cue the mysterious music of your choice). He has this way of presenting an understanding of the Enneagram personality system and then helping you see how to rest and destress well based on yourself and how you are wired. It is fascinating stuff. Mind you, I HATE... did I say that loud enough? I HATE personality stuff. I hate being put in a box and told how I am. But this stuff is accurate and doesn't put me in a box. It created some spaces that I have felt released in and understanding of myself. So yeah, it's a shameless plug for the man. Get his book and engage it. Learn yourself because the following parts will be the foundations for making earth-shattering changes in the world around you. It starts with you, though. You are the most essential character of your story. You are the hero of it. You are the one.

You heard me say moments ago that I was doing a few different jobs to make things happen. You don't have to be a professional and be paid to make a difference. So many times, we need to be paid to make the changes. That it is for a professional that we will get stuff done. Here is the reality check in it all. You don't have to be paid to make a difference. I am releasing you of that burden. The other thing is this. Social action, changing the world, making a difference, whatever label you put on it can and will become a lifestyle for yourself. Lifestyle is different from a career. Now, it could become your career, but it doesn't matter. I promise that if you embrace this attitude of seeing the need and filling it. Not waiting for someone else; your core being will be changed. You will be living out the golden rule of doing unto others as you want done unto you. It will become expressed and manifested in your daily life. See what happens if you get burdened. Your burden will drive you to acquire or find the skills needed to make things happen. You are the visionary. You are the one who has seen this need and has had thoughts of making it change. You are the one that was made for this.

I go back to the *Young Life* thing because when you are a youth worker in a town, your goal is to make a difference in kids' lives. To be that person who organizes spaces for students to unlock their infinite potential. I had this vision of students just going through life entirely. It is what I would want. It is what I had. So, with this, your heart is your biggest weapon. Your heart for this topic you have is the ultimate fuel. The desire to make it work is HUGE. All it takes is to view yourself as worthy of the task.

Donald Miller is a man who has shaped my organizational learning and life mission, and he has a book, "Hero on Mission". It's the other foundational book to read. As a matter of fact, I am going to say this. Ian Crohn with Donald Miller, and this book, you are set to have stories that will rival the ages. I know it's a bold claim, but as I write this down, I am excited about what will happen next for you. Okay, so let's keep charging ahead.

So, I mentioned Donald Miller in the last chapter. He wrote a book called Hero on a Mission. This thing is a must-read for all humans. I know that is a bold claim, but it is life-changing for every person I know who encounters it. This next section is a lot of his teachings expressed through me.

When I think about Donald Miller, he's always been someone who has impacted me in life. I remember the first time I watched Blue Like Jazz, and there were people's faces and voices of the characters of his book, or characters such as people in his book since it was a memoir. But there was this reality check for me in his book, the way he wrote and portrayed things; I felt like I was a part of those people. And I got to watch his life from an outside view. Many times over, his writings have been important to me in the sense of getting outside of my own eyes and looking at my world with a different camera angle.

He has this methodology called Story Brand. And he used it for a life system and even business. His recent book, "Hero on a Mission," has been imperative to my self-care journey. I want to express that his writing is not rocket science. But what he has done has put this all together in a very brief way. That is very important to the well-being of ourselves as we journey and break out of consumerism.

Miller prescribes that we, as humans, love a good story. And the fact is that we need to be embracing the fact that we are the hero in our story. The reality of this is that there are villains. A villain is against the hero versus the hero who is rising against the challenge or the villain. And then, he prescribes even further to dig into the psyche of a villain versus a hero, and so forth.

What I want to encourage you in this process is that when you become a victim, and the fact that you're even reading this book, you become a victim of the frustration of a problem in your community. Becoming a victim of that, then that... You'd have to rise above it or let the status change. Miller would say that when people let things go, they become more delved in their victimology to the point that they'll become a villain and want to ruin everybody else.

Miller also says that if you don't want to stay a victim, you must rise and become a villain or a hero. And what is impressive to me is that the side of this is that you rise to be the hero. And by reading this, you want to be a hero. You want to change the spaces around you. And you want to go after that. And the critical piece here is to understand that you will be stepping into a space that puts you into hero status. You will be stepping into a space no one else has entered. Or they have, and you'll be filming a fellowship, and we'll talk about that even later in the book what it means to gather that group up.

But I want you to understand that when you step out and become a hero, this is the first point that you are making a difference and taking a step that you want to see a change. And when you want to see that change happen. You're moving into hero status.

Miller also prescribes that every hero needs a guide, and the fact that you're even reading this book, I'm helping you be that guide on your journey. So I am your Gandalf to your Frodo or Obiwan to your Luke Skywalker. You pick it! You figure out the story you like, but you get the idea. And if I were a big Harry Potter fan, I could give you a Harry Potter reference. But that's for my children and not me. The only thing... Well, on a side note here, I'll let you know. The only thing I enjoy about Harry Potter is butterbeer. And I've had a lot of butterbeer in my time. And I find it delicious. I digress there just because I want you to understand there is something beautiful in stories.

And Miller's book "Hero on a Mission," I highly recommend it. I've used it in business, life, and nonprofit work. Because frankly, we need to understand that we were built... Humans were created with the love of a story. Now, with that, I want to nail down a couple of quick points for you that I would consider...

Well, I'll say it this way. A lot of times, we push ourselves past what we need to. We believe that we have to become it all. And the reality is that you need to become the hero of your story. That's it! It would be best if you focused on becoming the hero of your story. Many times over, we don't understand how to handle our schedules and how to manage our time. And I want you to be all in. And I mean that whole-heartedly. Be all in! Your lifestyle can be one of making changes. Your lifestyle can be just this one item.

My lifestyle has been community service for the past 15 years. And part of that over time, what I've learned in this short 2~3 years of these Aha-moments, is that it's all about the process and how we handle things. It's about how we operate. It's about who we have around us. It is about who we're looking up to and who we're bringing up.

See! Your heart is ideally placed to be the hero of the story. You are set. You have the knowledge and... How should I say this, the heart, the anger, the frustration? You have all those pieces needed right now to set on your journey of being a hero. And this is the critical factor. So, you're made for this. You were made for this. And you are the hero of your story right now by picking up this book. You have made this choice to rise above it. You're not a professional right now. You're just you! You're a hero! And you've moved past your consumeristic culture by wanting to make a change. So, with that, I can't wait to dive into the next chapter.

3

CULTURAL COMPASS: DECODING THE COMMUNITY GPS

I WANT you to realize how the world works around you. It's important to understand that you live in a community. And in the community, some things happen. And there are spaces that people exist in. And there are authorities over these spaces. And the reality is that you are not alone. So, with the understanding that you're not alone, I think it's so important to realize that, to own that you are working in a community system. Whether it's a local, regional, national, or international project you have. There are people around you.

So, I want to tell you three stories of three people who rose above and engaged in spaces that have just impressed me. The first person is Claire Moyer. Now, Claire Moyer, on the exterior, if you met him, you'd never realize that he is Gandalf. This man has so much wisdom because of the years he lived. And the fact is those lived-out years are fully lived. He lived with purpose. He lived with meaning. As Claire and I engaged in our community, one thing that stood out to me about him was he knew he was older. And he knew that he had wisdom to share with others. When I first met him, he sat on the porch of one of the projects. We were working on a volunteer house. And he had come to talk to me. And he told me how good I was. How great I was, and all the things he thought were terrific. But then, he also told me this was where I needed some help. I watched this gentleman step into my space with authority. And I received it. And the only authority I had with him was that he was a successful businessman. And in his retired years, he turned his heart towards ministry and mentoring.

Now, he was an average guy with a heart for business. He had had multiple businesses that he was a part of. He sold off a bus company that he rose to. And even in his later years, he continues to mentor business people. What Claire did for me, though, was beyond that. And during these times of self-care, one of the things that he taught me was receiving gifts. There were many times when Clair took care of me and my family during my missionary times when finances and things were tight. He ensured others were propping us up and participating in the solution. Claire was willing to take his time and still does. Even as I write this book, he and I have a beautiful relationship. Sometimes, he would say that I was mentoring him. And I'll say I'm mentoring... And he's mentoring me. But the reality is he has affected our community in so many ways. He's been a part of many social groups and taken action as a behind-the-scenes person propping up heroes. The biggest thing I can tell you about Claire and why I want to focus on this last part about him is this fact. He was willing to own that his life story was important. And it needed to be shared with me. And I can tell you right now. I wouldn't have gotten through this journey.

As a matter of fact, he was the one that got me into *Young Life*. And he did that by being very bold, and in my face, and asking me a series of questions. That put me on the defense, but then it ended up putting me into an offensive mode, where I wasn't looking to try to hold my ground but how to engage my ground. See! It's essential to have people like Claire Moyer in your life. And you need to look for them if you don't have them. Because Claire is that guy who rose above the consumeristic world. In his retirement years, he would probably say that he works harder, being retired, helping others, and moving around than he did when working. But his work is so important.

As I see it today, and the fact is that he's been a guide to me as the hero. And yeah! I can't express enough to you. As you're processing to look for someone like Claire, look for someone who's risen above the area, and approach them if they still need to come to you. Approach them about what you need, what you see in them, and how they can help you.

I could write a whole book on this next experience. I'm going to stick with a brief overview. And that's my best friend Craig's mom, Elaine. And Craig and I were close to each other. We had severe frustrations with a lot of things in the world. And we were teamed up to make a difference when we were in college. He was tragically taken from this Earth in a car accident I was a part of. I lived through it. He died. We were struck by a drunk driver. And it was over, our friendship here on Earth!

Losing someone, especially a friend, is epic and brutal. And when they're your best friend, you look at them like your little brother. It's definitely something that is a harsh reality. And I could write a whole book on just getting over the grief of losing a friend. And maybe that's another book I write, who knows. But here I sit telling you that Craig's Mom took her anger about drunk driving and went to another level. And she got a part of "Mothers Against Drunk Driving". And she took a stand. And I've watched this woman over the years take the stand and tell the story of her son, constantly engaging her community and ensuring that people understood that drunk driving is genuine. And it's a harsh reality when your child dies at the hands of someone else who made choices they shouldn't have made.

And so often, in our grief and pain of situations around us, we are called inside of us to rise, and we want to make a change. We want to make a difference. And I watched this woman, with her presentation, roam around and do her thing. She constantly engages people on this topic of drunk driving because the fact is this: a man one night made a wrong choice with alcohol that ended up killing my best friend and her son. And she and her husband, Tony, have made it a mission in their life to make a difference in others so that this tragedy doesn't happen to someone else. And again, I don't want to sit here and praise them for what they did. But I think it is a reality check to understand that.

Claire and Elaine, as they make their difference, are just ordinary human beings; Elaine was not a trained writer or presenter to step out and do these presentations. No! It was her heart and her passion that moved her to be there and stand with others. And I know through the years, she has touched lives. And people have talked with her and engaged with her. She wrote a book on Craig's life, A Faithful Servant, a note, and the book here for people to know what book it is, so they can read it and understand that her pain has been affecting so many other people's lives by standing up.

And I believe it's been a healing process for many as they journey through the tragedies of drunk driving. Remember, sometimes it's in our anger and pain that some of the most beautiful things are born. And it's also important to understand that when we have bad situations, we can make a difference afterward. This next person, Dick Fox, has been influential and essential in my life over the past eight years, as I write this, actually 11 years as I write this 10 years. Yeah, it will be 10 years. So, I needed to tell you the story of how I found Dick Fox or how Dick Fox found me. And it's imperative to understand this because he has guided me on a journey.

But that is ongoing. And we'll have this journey until we die. Dick would probably tell you the same as Claire did, that I'm a guide to him. And we live in the space of a 47-year-old man with a 70-ish-year-old man in my space. He has been an ongoing motivator and someone who has been able to engage me as a friend. And I'm saying all this more, in case he reads this book.

So you can see how awesome he is because he doesn't realize it some days. But also for you to understand that as I tell this story of Dick Fox, you will realize that he is someone of a character and nature that I think many people should rise to be. And Dick and I met one day. And you'll learn more about the community center and project process. And

I'll share more about that. Later in the book, in the steps... But Dick and I met over a renovation project. And we were building a counter. And the first day we met, the funny part about it was I was supposed to be the project manager that day running the shell. And we were there for a workday, and he was there with some friends. And as he and I started to engage in the project of building some counters, I got violently ill and had to leave. And he was left doing the work and finishing their project.

So, I was sick that week. We did a fantastic job of building some health board-certified counters. The joke is that I start the work, and then Dick finishes it. And that's how our relationship has been. Dick Fox is a man that took time in his life to travel, engage in spaces and do things that he dreamed of, and chase after his dreams. He's traveled around the country as a truck driver and auto mechanic. He has a love for bicycles. One day, he heard that I was working on a project around bicycles, and currently, I'm known for his bike and soul. And there'll be a book about that, I'm sure, coming soon.

But there was this fact that I had this passion to help kids work. I noticed a need for more space in our community to teach kids how to work in a job setting. He heard this plea of mine and wanted to build a bicycle program. And he was a bicycle mechanic by hobby and always wanted to do these things and work with students. So he and I got together! And over the years, we've forged the "Bike and Sol." And this process, this program grew and kept growing. And as it keeps growing and morphing from an after-school program into a full-on bike shop gaining national recognition... This man, with this not professional skill but a volunteer skill of bicycle mechanic, could touch so many lives.

First, he was my guide and taught me how to become a hero mechanic. And I've been building bikes. They've been used in auctions in many different spaces to earn money for nonprofits, assist people in their own lives, or bring joy to bicycling. But Dick was just taught so many students. I mean, probably, we've never really made the count of how many kids have come through with Dick. But we average about 4~5 students a week who are working regularly.

It's approximately 60 students a year that we affect through the shop and different levels. And there is this love that this man has for teaching, engaging, and imparting the knowledge of bicycle mechanics to those around him, adults and children. But the one thing that sticks out for me about Dick Fox that needs you to understand is that he could do so many things in his retirement. But instead, he spends three days a week in that bicycle shop, teaching, engaging, repairing, and dealing with humanity.

See, the thing is that when one retires, you have a choice to make whether you're going to give back and engage or hold steady and relax. See! We can ignore the world, or we can engage. And Dick Fox chose to engage the world regularly. And he's become a hero in his own story. But yet, at the same time, he has been guiding so many people in the art of bicycle mechanics. And you see a bicycle; this piece opens up doors. When you ride a bicycle, your mind and body come together synchronously. And it is an uplifting moment. It helps your body feel better. It helps your mind grow.

And the reality is that Dick Fox has helped so many people through his mechanical skills. Change your life. And it's important to realize that someone like yourself can take your skills and make a difference. And see, you need to hear all this because as you are rising above, as you are becoming that person that stands in that gap of the things that you want to stop or change, you need to realize that people like Craig, Elaine, and Dick, they didn't sit by and watch the world go by. Instead, they saw those spaces, stepped out, and had an impact. And they will never know the measure of their impact. They won't. It won't be counted for them. One day, they'll be able to see.

But the fact is that there might be a memoir or something written that they might get something. The truth is they will never know the actual full impact. And I want you to hear that it's not just me. And it's not just me stepping out on my own. But there have been people who have poured into my life as I run into others who have been able to make these things happen. And you're not alone. And as you understand your culture around you, and as we dig into this stuff, and what makes up a community, you need to be able to identify those people in your community that are rising above the culture and the fray, and that aren't being sucked into consumerism, and get close to them. And see that, I might be putting the cart before the horse. But I needed to tell the stories to you.

Because as we look at the spaces that people are going to that, as you look and understand who is around you and the roots of your problems and the situations that are going on, the stories that I tell you, there were people behind the scenes that were making this stuff happen for me that were building me up that were pushing me forward that were making me go to levels that I could never have experienced before in my life. And that's what is vital for us to remember: this journey that we're going on right now, these changes that we want to make, will go down through the ages. And generation after generation will be affected.

Because if we look at Claire... If we look at Elaine and we look at Dick. These three people, what they did, and how they stepped out have affected me, which has affected my own life, my children, the lives around me, and the thousands that have come in contact with me over the years in the work that I've done. And I need you to hear this. That's you. And as you start to learn and engage this stuff, I need you to understand that these are the pieces of life that will be so important for you to grab hold of and know that... How do I say this? Know that you are going to make a change of epic proportion, and whatever space you're in, it will make a difference in people's lives and impact on the Earth. And the ripple effect is enormous.

Do you know what? Just do a lesson for life: grab a stone, go out onto a clear speck of water, throw one stone into the water, and see what it does. One pebble, and watch the ripple. But then, go and grab a whole bunch of those small stones, grab a bunch of them, and throw them in the water.

Watch the waves that start to happen. I remember a time when I was at Camp Medellin. And I was speaking to an outdoor school of students. And there are approximately 50~60 kids there. And I asked them all to throw stones into the water. As they threw the stones and the pebbles into the water, representing their lives, the wave started the forum on the pond. And there was this reality check that as we engage in our community, as we understand this culture around us and our community culture, you must get this and feel this concept that says you will make an impact. And you're going to have a story. And your story is going to affect others. So, let's dig in now! I hope you're feeling motivated. I hope you're feeling encouraged. And we will start looking at this stuff that makes up our communities.

People exist in 3 different types of spaces. These places are where humans hang out. Work, play, relax, basically do life. Where do you live? What spaces do you go to that show you the trail you wander on? Many times over and over, we move in our lives, and we don't pay attention to where we are going. See, the reality is you exist. The spaces that you live in are significant. Think about where you are in a week. What are those places? If I was to look at my life, it would center around my home. Then I have my job place and places I volunteer. Finally, you have the spots that I am entertained at and shop. These are the main places most of us travel in a week. We like to have our spaces of home, work, and play. Now, shopping can be considered play or work, but it is more like play as it is a fun place to venture to. Of course, if you are online shopping, that doesn't count. Also, if you spend time in video gaming and virtual worlds, that could be considered a 4th type of space or community in your mind. Still, it would be a gathering place for entertainment, just like the movie theater or sports arena. It's home entertainment since you don't leave home. We will focus on the 3 main spaces for our plans and this writing. Home, Work, and Play. I want to look at these in their significance and tell some stories about them and why it's essential to understand these spaces about community development work. Also, why are they so important to you as you solve the problems around you?

The first space is home. Home, for me, has always been my sanctuary. It is the place I go to for my rest. My home provides me with that base of operation. Homelife can get messy at times, but in the end, it is the space we occupy where the heart of our life happens. Home life can often be a basis for tragedy and hardship. I remember doing youth work in Schwenksville. One of my student's homes could have been better. It was not a space of rest but a place of turmoil. The student did everything he could not to be at home. He would spend time outside to escape the inside. This is different from how things should be. Home should be a first space. A place that brings us joy and development. As we become an adult, we form our own homes. We create a new space that is our principal place of dwelling. The home creates a nurturing environment for ourselves. It is the place that we launch from daily. From our 1st space of home space, we undertake to our second space.

Work is what we, as humans, were built to do. Weekly, most of our culture heads off to their jobs. Now, some folks work from home as we see more and more since the days of COVID. The fact is we have workplaces. Spaces created for us to earn an income and move forward in life. We look at these spaces as a hub for our economic growth. It is a place where our relationships are engaged around what? Work. The workplace space aims to foster relationships and an environment for work to flourish and be created to earn an income. Work can take on many forms to people. It can be enjoyable but also arduous and grueling. One job for one person may be life-giving while another is life-draining. A reality around all this stems from the workplace being a source of tension and satisfaction. Humans love to do a good job. They appreciate being praised and acknowledged for their deeds. The workplace is a crucial environment for all that exists in the world. Even if you are a retired person, the workplace could look different. It could be a spot you volunteer at. Even volunteer spaces could be work. Work is that space that you extend yourself to accomplish a task or goal when it's all said and done. We need to acknowledge and understand that workplaces exist throughout our communities. Hubs for economic growth make up a large part of our infrastructure. It is through the workplaces that many parts of community life extend. If we look at the fabric of a community, the tax base comes from the reality that people are working. Most of their wages are gifted to the local, regional, and state governments and, finally, our Federal government. Time and time again, we do not look at our workplaces as part of the community. Many times, it's overlooked because, well, it's my job. Yet, in these spaces, many of us identify who we are and our role in this world because of our jobs.

Finally, we have our play spaces. These are the spots where people can enjoy themselves. We go to these spots to have fun and let go of the work day. Third, spaces can have dual roles as places we may take work colleagues to. Still, in the end, the purpose of space is to enjoy yourself and not necessarily work the traditional job roles. One of my favorite third spaces is coffee houses. Others may call them cafes. In my town of East Greenville, there was a coffee shop called Java Good Day Cafe. It was amazing. I stepped into the space soon after I started renovating the community center I was working on.

I asked the proprietor at the time, Ann if I could use a table as an office when they were open. She kindly said yes and even gave me bottomless coffee. See, I would meet and engage people in that space daily and month after month. Java turned into my 3rd space. Sure, was I getting work done there? Yes, but it did not exist for my job. The reality is that Java was a social hub in our community. Daily, I would see people that I needed to talk to. Everyone from people dealing with newborn issues to soldiers handling wounds from war. Step by step, the place grew on me, and day by day, I kept eating and drinking there. The space has grown, and a musical stage was put in. I, too, have a musical stage in our building. It does beg to ask the more profound questions. I wondered why I kept coming back to the space. 3 owners later and a third name change, I am still there. The same guy is doing the same thing. It is my space. I enjoy it. I relax and talk about life with people from all walks of life. It is a place where everyone can join in. It is a 3rd space.

These spaces we talk about are crucial to understanding what it means to engage our community. So, with that, let me break down the community center process. As we talked to the school board, they had issues with teenagers needing things to do. See, there were no third spaces that were teen-conceive. We had some restaurants, but that was about it. A couple of youth ministries at churches and sports teams existed, but that was for a particular type of student. For the broader student population, we did not have anything. We had to investigate and understand the spaces leading up to student issues. Lacking in 1st, 2nd, and 3rd spaces, a human can end up in a negative spot. A place that can bring them down and ultimately lead to suicide. It is having positive spaces for people to engage in that matters.

So, what do your spaces look like for the problem you are solving? Is it something that centered around homelife? Workplace issues? A need for spaces to relax and unwind? Where do people hang out in these spaces? If you are going to solve your problem, where do the people you work with exist according to these spaces? For 1space -where do people live? What are the neighborhoods in your region? Who lives in them? What do they do there? Are you a bedroom community? That is a place.

People only sleep in their town and head out for work and entertainment. Are you rural? Rural suburban? Suburban? Metro? How do people live? What types of homes? Single townhouses, row homes, small land plots? These dynamics play into what the community threads are like in the spaces where people live. If you are trying to make an impact, you need to understand where people live and why. Are there economic systems at play? Are specific neighborhoods problematic and could be the source of your issue? So many factors play into issues, but understanding where people live is part of the puzzle.

Where are the places people work? Businesses can often be a source of support and resources as you go about your work. Understanding what businesses exist and how they interact with the community is super important because those businesses may last longer than some of your residents. Many businesses also care about the community because it is where their employees dwell. Factories, stores, services, manufacturing centers, the list goes on and on about businesses. Understanding who owns them. Where are they headquartered? Where do they donate, and what causes are they funding? Knowing who the businesses are may also create an allie list for you. Knowing who is capable or willing to engage in your mission is crucial to a long-standing engagement. So often, it is a flash in the pan when we don't have the proper partners around us. Knowing who is working in these places and where they are coming from can give you a leg up in understanding who is in your community.

Finally, the 3rd space is where people will hang out. Restaurants and entertainment spots are at the top of the list. This can be parks and recreational areas as well. Essentially, it is wherever someone would go to unwind and relax. Third, spaces show the heartbeat of a community. Seeing how a community unwinds will then open our doors to the possibilities of how people enjoy their excess time. What do people do for fun in your community, and why? If a community is tied to the outdoors, solutions based on the outdoors may be meaningful. Urban settings tend not to have such a strong tie to the land as rural do. Suburban is a mix, as it should be because it combines urban and rural. When it is all said and done, the ultimate fact remains that a third space is where people will go to melt away the stress of the day that isn't their home. Third spaces are also where people spend their recreational capital and focus on the money that they earn in the workplace and do not need to hold onto for their home life. This creates another view of economics around these spaces and their impact on your community.

Knowing where people live, work, and play will get you to understand your community. Engaging in these spaces will only strengthen your foundation to make real change.

WHO ME? YES, YOU!

4

ROOTS UNVEILED: DIGGING
DEEPER, SHERLOCK STYLE

We have identified a problem, and the pace at our community exists. You heard stories of people stepping up and going the extra mile. Now, it's time to dig into what is the root of your issue at hand. When we look at this issue, we need to understand where it comes from and who has authority in the spaces around us to solve it. Problems can be small, medium, large, and just humongous. It doesn't matter what size the problem is, as much as knowing where it started. Who are the stakeholders and authorities in the spaces where the issues lie? Then you can make up a plan.

I remember a young girl named Shannon. She was attending the youth ministry I was overseeing at the time. She has a string of life issues. Mental health was at the top of the charts, and she wrestled with borderline personality disorder. This disorder comes with many symptoms and various ways to handle it. BPD is brutal, to say the least. It stems from a tragedy in someone's life and its not-so-pleasant effects on them. If the crisis is not treated, BPD can set in. It creates strong pulls of disobedience and such. It is a mess to deal with inside someone's being. Their self-worth lowers, and depression can kick in, as well as self-harm and suicide.

Truth be told, I have experienced it many times with various teens. It is always a challenging situation. In this case, Shannon had some real struggles. Her 1st space was home. It was not a good place. She lived in a basement apartment with her mother and sister and her mom's boyfriend. The apartment was in the basement of her grandmother's house. Grandma and other family members who lived upstairs had issues with drugs. Shannon's mom, Martha, had her own set of issues. She was struggling with Multiple Sclerosis MS, and it was crippling her. She also had a former addiction to Meth, which negatively affected her mind. Overall, the home was severe. Very tough. She also was molested by her mother's boyfriend when she was a young girl. This trauma was a significant factor in her developing BPD.

The second space for her was school. Since she didn't work, school would be that space. She would travel to school 5 days a week, creating an escape from home. In school, she had some friends and had to work on relationships with them. The tension around her was great. The school was a small escape from the significant problems at hand. Her depression was evident as she walked the halls and engaged with her teachers. Shannon was hurting, and it was seen in her 2nd space.

The third space was a youth group and friends' houses. There was only so much else for a teenager to do in that town. It was a small town with a park and a library, plus a restaurant for people to go to. The 3rd spaces were not present. See, this is also a factor when we lack third spaces. It's hard for people to unwind and let go. The struggle I saw was that more and more teens like Shannon kept coming into my space. The mental health problems among students were so significant that I had to start realizing that home life, school, and lack of third space would not give much hope to someone like Shannon. A new environment must be created.

Noticing these issues with Shannon, it was clear she didn't have a third space to thrive and release the negative energy around her. Many times, in situations, a lack of third space is what is the issue. The root of the problem for Shannon was her home life. Life at home was causing her to break down and struggle with life in her 2nd and 3rd spaces. The root of the issue stemmed from the first space. Understanding this meant that a change in the 1st space was needed for more change in her life. Changing the space creates a way for her to thrive. The problem was now identified, and the spaces required to change were known. Home was the priority. Working at home life would then improve her 2nd space in the school.

I can't begin to express the reality of what it is when identifying spaces. For Shannon, the spaces are a significant influence in her life. Time and time again, we see that space influences us for good or bad. For Shannon, the reality was that her school space was a significant factor in her life. Friends, teachers, and the pressures of school continue to be a factor for any student as they walk out into the world. When we saw that her first space being home was not an easy fix, we moved on to focusing on the mentality at school. This created a new reality that her 3rd space needed to be addressed. Her third space was the places she roamed. Positive or negative, the reality of the third space engages us beyond.

3rd space for her was the youth group ministry she attended with us and roaming around town. Friends houses as well. Understanding that her home was the problematic location and school was affecting her deeply, we wanted to key in on the 3rd spaces to improve them and address what else was needed in the long run. Once you see things, it goes easy, but it doesn't. I had countless interactions with her, her mother, and authorities in her spaces. The reality is that it took a lot. I mean a lot. I will pause there, and let's look at your issue or issues you are addressing. What are those roots?

The root of a problem is simply this. Where does it start? When looking at any situation, you must look at the base issue. For instance, someone comes to me and says they are unsheltered and out of work. I began to ask the probing questions. Here is a list of questions I run through:

- What is the main issue?
- What was the road to this place? What was the journey taken that got to this problem?
- Who are the characters of this story?
- Who or what is the villain in this situation?
- If there is a villain, how did the villain come to be?
- What resources are not being utilized to fuel a solution?
- What resources have been depleted to make the solution happen?

These quick hits start us out in a place of launching. When we can see the root, we need to identify it and understand what can be done to kill it. Right? As a plant grows and weeds come around it, what are those weeds, and how do we eliminate them? Some weeds get pulled and poisoned, starve out sunlight and water, and die off.

Using the plant analogy, we think about the weed and how we pull it. Typically, for most weeds, you reach in and remove it. Boom, done, problem solved. Other weeds need some suitable, hearty gloves on to pull them out. Or, maybe a big ol shovel, and you dig it out, and it's gone.

Some weeds are very ground-covering and have deep roots that are those types. Not a simple pull or dig will cut it. They need to be poisoned, right? Laying out the poison and watching them die off slowly. Taking the time to kill them and ensure they don't come back.

Covering up the ground in plastic also is a preventative or killing process. When a new flower bed starts, you clear it out by removing the potential growth by laying plastic and starving the sunlight. This prevents weeds from sprouting and engaging. The same thing happens when solving a problem. We need to identify all the surrounding weeds or villains engaging our story. Time and time again, something is always at the root of the issue. Many times, with unsheltered issues or lack of work, mental health is a huge factor. Understanding where someone's journey has been helps identify those weeds and how we get to the bottom.

I want to go down a rabbit trail for a moment or have a sidebar about mental health and humans. I wish someone told me early in my community development career that mental health is a messy weed to root out. It isn't something that is permanently eliminated. Chemical or social imbalance is the root of it, and understanding where that comes from is so important. For instance, social or personality disorders have been picked up and taught in an unhealthy fashion. It could be negative coping skills due to trauma or a whole other list of behaviors that can occur due to insufficient parenting and environments to grow up.

Chemical imbalance is precisely that. An imbalance physically that can be adjusted with medication. Other poor coping skills can be managed by meds as well. Still, in the end, it is essential to realize that when you start engaging in negative social behaviors with someone, you need to check on them. See, many times over, we are taught to know if our physical body is off; we get it checked out by ourselves, at an ER, or by a primary care physician. We have these different levels to help out as we see the severity of the situation. It is essential to realize that we, too, can have some first aid practices for someone hurting due to mental illness symptoms. Learning more from whomever you are working with is very important to understand their journey. Where and to whom they have seen and gone to. What are they lacking in resources to address this situation?

Regarding all this, I want to let you understand that life is essential. When dealing with people and their root problems, you need to consider that someone is trusting you with their life and their understanding of their vulnerable situation. These realities are what make us as we become the guide in their story. They are the hero that we want to make and grow. People's problems are on a different scale than community issues, but they can still be handled the same.

For instance, if we look at the macro issue of unsheltered, we can run through our question list and get some answers depending on what town or area you are dealing with. For example, there is often a need for more resources to assist someone to get out of their unsheltered issue. Unsheltered people that I have engaged with have made or been a victim of bad choices. A series of events have come about, and they have lost the ability to the proper resourcing that is needed to adjust in their space appropriately to live. It could be broken down transportation always to lack of appropriate medical care for their health that kept them from work. In the end, a reality check has to happen, and we are the ones that need to understand the root of the problem. It is through the root that we can solve the issue at hand.

Now, I know sometimes symptoms can look like the root of the problem. It is easy to say someone is unsheltered because there is a need for jobs in the area. Well, staying in one town isn't the issue; most people can have access to work somewhere. It is something else deeper for that person. See, getting past the symptoms and getting to the root is essential. Think about the weed and plant analogy. A low-growing weed may be running through a garden. At a glance, it looks nice, and its aesthetics are great for the garden. But, in the soil, the weed is stealing nutrients that the plants you want to grow cannot have. The symptoms could be handled with more fertilizer. The fact is yes. You could address the symptom of a lack of nutrients by more fertilizer. If you investigate a little deeper, the problem is the weed itself. Many times, our root problem is hidden behind symptoms.

Humans are notorious for throwing money at problems to solve the symptoms. If someone doesn't have a place to live, we give them money; if they have housing, they will be okay. This may create a stopgap but will not address the main root problem.

Ask the questions and dig deeper. Look at what is going on and what are the spaces involved. Is it a home issue? Work issue or entertainment issue? Where are the problems coming from, and how do you get into those spaces to solve them? Time and time again, we need to realize that these spaces that we tread in can create the answers we need to what we are dealing with. Identifying where the problems are coming from can give us a reality check on the whole thing.

Shifting a moment, I want to do another sidebar. This is in regards to handling a trauma. Sometimes, traumas present themselves, and we must address them here and now. The trauma may become a new root of an issue or a symptom of a more significant problem. Either way, trauma is something that drastically affects someone negatively. You see, traumas are handled in two ways by someone. They run from it and escape, or they address it head-on. Traumas have a way of cropping up in the journeys and can be masked as the root. Granted, they may be the root of another issue, but I would instead think of this as a vine. For instance. Going back to Shannon. A trauma happened in the journey of getting her to a healthy and thriving state in life. In this process, she experienced a break into their apartment. All of her coping mechanisms were stolen regarding electronics. This was devastating. It also warranted a visit by the police. Imagine if you could be a middle school girl having your room broken into and everything was gone. Then, come to find out, they broke in and started from a door into your living space attached to your extended family upstairs. WOW right? Your own family broke in and stole your stuff. The things that help you get through the night.

I was called to the scene, and the police asked me to address some living situations. In this conversation, we find out it is, I mean, awful upstairs. There was no evidence of anything the police could do, but they wanted me to get the girl and her mother out that night. They felt it could be unsafe for their long-term well-being.

The trauma was presented, and that one instance is just a moment in time. I had to then work immediately on finding shelter short and long-term. This trauma was not just a singular event but the primary weed being the home life situation. Therefore, as we look at our questions, we can say that she and her mother needed short and long-term stay spaces. The short term was my family's home for the girl, and a single woman in our church was able to house the mother that night. Then, the long-term solution was that the woman would keep her mom and daughter longer term as residents in her condo. This short- and long-term game approach helped me deal with the trauma. I addressed it and looked at it for a long-term solution.

Traumas will happen around you. If you step into them, be the guide, and look at the situation, you can help redeem it. Moment by moment, you can engage and move forward. Looking to be the calm in the chaos in those small moments. By identifying resources and looking at where the vine is growing from, you can engage it quickly and then get back to the main issue.

The spaces are essential when we look at who is in charge of those spaces. See, realizing that we can make change, we also have to look at who are the gatekeepers to the change. For instance, first space issues can result from family system issues. Therefore, in a family structure, we must look at who influences the situation. This could be a spot.

There are two types of authority that we see in our spaces. Positional and Relational. Positional authority is based on the position someone carries. A boss, a police officer, a judge, a business owner, a landlord, a father, a mother, a teacher, a board member, etc... I think you get it. It's pure and simple: someone has authority because they are the ones who gain control of resources because of what they do. These positional authorities are in a place of power just because of what they do, not necessarily who they are.

Relational authority comes from a space of who someone is concerning the situation. Relational authority happens because of the interactions of humans. The relationship that is given can create authority in one's space. Relational authority is much harder to identify because it takes time to interview and understand who is involved in the different spaces. Knowing that we people are engaged in our situation can create a better understanding of who has influence and can be a gatekeeper of resources needed to get the job done.

So, we see who these people are and how we need to interact with them. Understanding t that positional authority may bring a more profound and procedural process than dealing with someone relationally. I do not want to negate that relationships, even within a positional authority, can happen. For instance, just because someone is a parent doesn't mean they have as much authority as possible if they do not have a good relationship with a child. If we go back to the Shannon story. Her mother had positional authority. There were certain things I could not help with or get resources handled unless Mom was willing to sign off on them. Simultaneously, the relationship between the mother and daughter was very fragmented, and Shannon had no relational authority regarding her mother. She loved her mom but did not respect her. She cared about Mom but did not value her advice or wisdom in her life.

Understanding the authorities' roles in our situations is vital to having the resources needed to solve the problems. Knowing who these authorities are will only enhance what you are doing. Understanding these authorities and what is happening is crucial to everything we do. I mean this.

It was a simple meeting. A bunch of pastors getting together for lunch and having the usual chats. How are things going in their churches? What was the latest hot topic of the day for sermons? I remember vividly sitting there as we were being served a 3-course meal at the local retirement community, that it all was a sham. The anger was inside me as I kept thinking about the student that took his life. It was just banging around inside me. Over and over, I am here, and he is not. I can make a difference. As we went around sharing, it hit me so hard to say it. I let it out about my pain, "Is anyone else broken up about suicide? I am so tired of people not having hope! Is anyone else hurting over this?" I knew they were. I knew the pastor of the child. He was a great friend... but I knew he felt helpless sometimes. We all do. We have those moments where we feel like we can't move on. Slowly, around the room, we began to share our pain over the situation and that we needed a change. We needed to go to the powers that be and ask the questions that needed to be asked. We had to go to the School District Administration. They were the ones that held the keys to the students. Right? They had families, local organizations, the faculty and staff, and the students all in their authority. We decided to move forward and look for solutions involving the school district.

When identifying those around us in authority, we must look at who we are trying to help. Who are the victims, so to speak, in the situation? Then, just as if you were looking up the food chain in nature, who is over them? Looking at a student, we would say a student. Then, as we group from there, we see parents, teachers, and any organizations they may be a part of. For the moment, for simplicity's sake, we will look at the concept that students answer to schools and parents. Some would also attend a church or be involved in some town activity. Still, the brunt of their life is under the authority of a school or a parent or guardian. In this reality check, we can see who has authority and where. Positional or relational is the other key. Now, parents do have authority positionally, but it is in the relationships that the absolute authority lies. Schools carry a positional authority. Students must go to school, or they and their parents could be fined and dealt with in court. It is a reality check that these entities hold positional authority. Teachers can create a relational authority as well in a student's life. We do not want to say relational authority happens without a position. It can be earned in a practical setting, but the access would still be positional. Understanding where these are coming from now creates the start of our tree.

The next step for the students and the teachers would be the principals, the administration, and finally, the school board. In our school district, a student's life would be teachers, guidance counselors, principals, administration, and ultimately the school board. This would be the school tree. By identifying this tree, we can see what steps we need to take to make a change. Now, hear me on this. Once we have identified these people, it is then and only then that we can make a change. When we look at these positions now, we can then take a step and identify what we are looking to do.

What is the solution that we are seeking? In his book Business Made Simple, Donald Miller says we need to have a simple 3-step process that will make a solution for our hero. In the case of our suicide and bringing hope to students, it was a simple task. Students who need hope should meet up with some adults who care about them to bring hope into their lives. It seems simple. That's because it is. We often need to break down our situations into the least common denominator. For instance, if there are issues with unsheltered people in an area. Unsheltered people need to be engaged in a place that can house them and set them back on their feet with the tools they need to survive. This will then set them off into the world thriving. Again, 1 2 3. What is the need? How do we solve it? What does it look like on the other end as success?

What is your problem? And what does it look like? Let's go deeper now with the solution. In steps 1, 2, and 3, for my students needing hope, we want to look at those in authority and ask more profound questions. For instance, what are the needs of students? What do they need to feel empowered to live a hopeful life? So, we mapped out the need to talk with the school district. We mapped out the reality that the most significant thing we needed to understand came from the school district themselves. They held the keys as professionals to the deeper hows and whats that we needed to know. What will the solution then look like? Do we understand that our solution looks like a student that is vibrant in life? They are engaged in thriving and moving ahead in life. Spending time in healthy relationships and seeing that they are enjoying the life they are living despite obstacles that come their way. Ultimately, the questions we ask are the ones that get us to the destination of our issues. We want a moment to identify the result and have a place where those in authority have given us the fundamental ideas it will take to make our solution happen.

In the end, it is open-ended questions that need to be asked. What do you feel is the need? Who can help? Who else should we talk to? Time and time again, it is about opening yourself up to partner with those in authority. It is then, through these steps, that you will see a clear path to your solution. The second step is the bigger one in steps 1, 2, and 3. Step one is finding/ recruiting, and step 2 is the execution of what you do. Step 3 is how you measure the success. These are also baselines for you to talk about with those in authority of your situation. What does a student look like when they are hopeful? What does a thriving, sheltered person look like? Time and time again, we need to measure and see that we are having success and know where we may need to improve our situation. When it is all said and done, you should understand what you need to know when meeting with those in authority who can make a difference and change the situation.

We will now dig into the more profound issue regarding authority and those who can help. Get ready for a deep dive into community relationships and development.

5

COMMUNITY METAMORPHOSIS: A
WHOLISTIC ROLLERCOASTER

AT THE END of the last chapter, I felt the tension and the reality that
there was an issue and others must have thought about it. As a set of
pastors in a town, we needed to make a change. It could be talked
about and something done. At that time, we decided to approach the
school district administration, get to the bottom of what was happening, and figure it out. I knew a 3 step process was it, but how we got
there was another ball game. About 6 of us gathered with the school
district superintendent, the high school vice principal, and the middle
school vice principal. The purpose was to discuss the issues at hand. I
remember that day because I was nervous. I was a 30-something who
thought he had all the answers to a problem but didn't know how to
solve it. I knew there were plenty of models, but this was my town.
These were my neighbor's kids. This was a whole different level. In
reality, I was sitting with the kings and queens of our education system.
We opened up and introduced ourselves, and then it happened. We, the
clergy, asked what were the top 3 issues they felt were stopping kids
from having hope. What needs must be fulfilled to create a space for
kids to have hope? I thought answering this would take a while, but the
3 made it very clear. It was rather remarkable. The idea was a program
that taught hope. Something that kids could come to and learn about

life and have adults care about them. There needed to be a space open to students in the public to go to and call their own. Finally, a new nonprofit is required to help with the community issues. There needed to be something that existed to bring all this together. Resources from around the community. I WAS SO EXCITED INSIDE! I knew how to build a program. For 15 years of my life, I was involved in thriving youth ministries. Pulling students off the streets gives them space to call their own.

I knew this, and I knew it well. Granted, I always did it in churches. They kept talking and bouncing around ideas of what a space would look like. Again, I felt I needed to say something, but I just listened. I kept listening and letting them talk about the topics, and others asked more questions. The conversation came to a halt, though, when the topic of a unifying nonprofit. See, that was something nobody in the room had experience in. Sure, we did youth programs and operated in various buildings, but nobody here had experience.

I was thinking back to a book I read. A local pastor taught me details about the seven mountains of authority in the community. He was in the room, too... He was happy with me as I stood up and detailed our community. I grabbed the marker and went to the whiteboard. I drew out 7 circles spread out in a circle around the board. Then I wrote on each circle the following labels: Education, Government, Business, Nonprofit, Media, Entertainment, Religion. I then put a circle in the center and drew lines like spokes out to them all. I told them how we, as a community, had these regions and needed a nonprofit to sit between them all.

Coordinating the community's needs and engaging on different levels ways to make it all better. That entity could sit in the center and coordinate efforts and resources to solve issues like this. A community center with programs for students and those that would engage in it would be coming from all these community sectors. I remember feeling so proud of myself. I had done it. I created a map of what needed to happen. I marked it all out, and everyone agreed. Everyone said it was great! We dismissed the school district, and we, as pastors, sat there. Everyone was satisfied that we knew what we needed to do...of course, who would lead it? Nobody had the time, but somebody needed to show it. I stood up and said I would do it. I knew in my heart of hearts I was called to solve this problem, and we had come this far. We just had a blessing from the educational authority to make this happen. So we continued on our journey...

It was simple. When you think about a community as a holistic entity with different parts, it makes solving problems in a community much more accessible. You can see who has what influence on the situation. You can understand who you need to talk to and their capabilities. Let's dig into these seven different areas and note their purpose and what resources they bring to your table.

Education: We start with this because all of us in the United States engage with the educational area of our community. Education is the centering authority on the development of students from Kindergarten to their senior year in high school. The education area has resources focused on developing students into well-rounded individuals in society regarding work and community interactions. There are spaces not only for skills to work but also for life and fun. Sports, hobby clubs, the arts, and the list goes on are activities that are centered around a student to explore and see who they are. All the while meeting the standards of an educational system that is governed by the state you live in. Education also can be beyond the senior year if you have colleges and universities or trade schools in your community. Where I am from, we do not have higher education directly in my town, but at a county level, we do. Realizing that education is a place that gives you direct access to students and families. Many times, Education is where you start when it comes to affecting families and students directly in a situation you would be encountering. It also could be a space for volunteers. Many student projects and groups focus on voluntary service that could be put into your volunteer force. Never discount the power of a child who wants to make a difference.

Government: It is what it is. I want you to distinguish the term government from politics. Politics has nothing to do with dealing with the government. You heard me. Politics is a whole other topic and shouldn't be a process you engage in as a community developer. When you look at your government entities, these are the people who are in positions that have authority and resources within their positions. It doesn't matter who gets elected. These people are the ones you work with. I say this because you may disagree with the politics but must work with them. So often, we let our political views get in the way of working with those around us. Government can be a lot of different layers: police departments, mayoral offices, borough councils, township supervisors, county officials, state officials, federal officials, etc... The list can go long and wide when it comes to the government. You have all these facets of community works, parks and recreation, and so forth, and so on. Sometimes, a task force could also be related to your specific area. Understanding the government in your community space is crucial. Please get to know them. Take them out for a coffee. Introduce yourself and what you are working on.

Find out who in the government may be directly related to the issues. For me, you saw how I went to education. The government people that I went to for a community center were the mayor, the zoning supervisor, and the police department that I was working with. These people had the authority to build and engage students directly. Mayors are typically the spokespersons of the town; they should have a pulse, and the zoning supervisor should have a pulse on what can or can't be built. What building or park resources may be available? Finally, the police know where the more profound problems are. They may have experienced the people that you wanted to engage with. In the end, the government has the public resources and finance that could assist.

Business: Exactly what it is. Who are the businesses in your town that have resources or care about what you are doing? It could start with the Chamber of Commerce as a way to know businesses. Maybe you take time to visit and engage different storefronts. Get to know the people there and how they can be a part of what you do. Some businesses might have the resources that you are looking for. I would need space and materials, possibly people, to help renovate. Food to feed the kids at times and equipment to engage them with. See, it is in the businesses that you can find ways to go deeper. You may even find that some businesses cross over into other community mountains. It could also be a space that you can connect and assist with. Those you are engaging could be new customers or employees of those you will build relationships with. Get to know those in business and what you are working on. Find those who want to partner.

Nonprofit: These are organizations that are devoted to a specific mission. It is in this mission that they are organized to get something done. This could be social service groups, pet shelters, community centers, and places focused on topics to make a change. Nonprofits may already engage in the spaces you want to help in. You may even become tied to them closer and closer than you might have been before. We are looking at this from a specific lens that you want to build bridges so when the time comes, you know who you can turn to for help, or they can turn to you for help. Nonprofits are influential because many are run by volunteers, and they have a zealous spirit to get solutions done.

Media: Who are the gatekeepers of communicating in your town? This includes newspapers, radio, television, and social media influencers. Many times, every town is different in how it operates. Understanding where the news goes and what people are reading is crucial for getting the word out. Also, Media is how you can learn the pulse of how people listen to the world around them. Social Media has given us the power to engage. However, we need to identify what sources are and what will matter. A national podcast, for instance, on your topic may be a great way to find others who can help with ideas or resources but may not provide boots on the ground. The local newspaper may be a great way to recruit volunteers. Knowing how your community uses and manages media will significantly enhance your efforts to get the word out.

Entertainment: Where do people go to relax and enjoy life? In these spaces, you can fundraise. Local restaurants, gyms, family fun centers, movie theaters, etc... are great spaces to partner and engage to get the word out and find funding. Sometimes, places host nights where a certain amount of the proceeds will go to causes. Entertainment also is a great way to meet people and build awareness of what you are doing.

Religion: Knowing the religious centers is essential. Where do people look outside the world for that higher calling to their lives? Religion can open doors for volunteer, financial, and resource partners. Religious centers often provide space and opportunities to do things that would not exist in other spaces. Partnering with religious institutions can bring a different kind of zeal than you would find in other sectors. Take the time to know the religious leaders of your community.

Understanding each of these mountains that our communities are built upon will only enhance the methods in which you work. Knowing who and what they bring to the table gives you people and resources and sets you up for how you will build a crew and set sail with everyone to get it done. Let's jump into the next chapter and see how you will be Jack Sparrow and grab the crew for the Black Pearl!

6

———

ALLIES ASSEMBLE: TEAMING UP FOR A CHANGE BINGE

STANDING before a high school auditorium filled with students. I got to the microphone and stood there in the hustle and bustle of their murmurs, and it was time to let out a war cry. I had to say something to grab their attention to listen to me. Something that would get them to pause and maybe maybe listen to what I had to say.

"GOOD MORNING! My name is Scott Roth, and who do you think I am?"

There was silence. You could see the look on their faces; they were like, what? I was asking them to label me. To look at my 6'3 burly exterior, all dressed in black with a bushy goatee and bald head and leather boots and jeans to label me. Sure, they label each other daily, as we all do in humanity, but I wanted them to let it all out.

"Biker dude"

"Nope, I ride a scooter"

And the labels kept flowing back and forth, letting them have fun with it, and eventually, someone yelled, "Pastor!"

"I don't look like a pastor."

Laughter ensued.

"But... I am one."

I let out a belly laugh. I then began to tell them about identity and talked to them about the pain I know they go through in life. Finally, I closed with a war cry. It's a war cry to step up and not live in mediocrity. Not to let others back down. In my story about the community center, I was given an old church building to use for free as a community. I also was given a platform at the school to run an after-school program for a year in the cafeteria while we renovated the building. It was epic! Right? I had this chance to stand before these students and cast a vision of change. A building to remodel and an after-school program to engage them and give them refuge. That was the name of it: "Refuge". It was on that day I found the start of my crew.

I knew that students would be the most effective crew to start with. They were the ones who lost their friend to suicide. They were the ones who walked the halls of the school and saw the pain. They were the ones that it was their friends that they could affect every day. I didn't want adults right away. I wanted students. I picked them, and on that day, I started to recruit. I told them what the issue was. It was that they needed a space to call their own. A place that was theirs to engage and for them to speak into. A place for them to have outside of school and their house. Remember 3rd spaces? Without teaching, I just taught them 1, 2, and 3 space areas! You see, I needed them to see the need. I needed them to understand that they all wanted that place. I had to name the problem. Naming the problem was step 1. Again, this is a nod to Donald Miller and his Story concepts.

Second, I began to tell them how I needed students to help work the building. To come and refurbish it with me. I had a second assembly where I was able to articulate that more. 2 assemblies telling students about the problems and what it was going to take to make it happen. I kept telling the students repeatedly that we would build a place they could go to and become better, and the world would improve.

After naming the problem and how we would solve it, I asked them to sign up! I gave them two spaces to engage me and get this project done. The first was with the senior class and their mentor program. The idea was to have seniors head into the community, work with nonprofits, and get things done. It was at that moment that I realized students wanted these, too. I had 7 seniors sign up that first semester and started working with me. Painting, Building, and creating a legacy on the property. We kept engaging the senior program for 8 years till COVID hit. It was amazing watching these students flow in and out, and their lives changed because of the work they were doing on the property.

When you create a vision, you have to name the problem. Express it very succinctly. I keep going back to Donald Miller and his work because his Storybrand concept of being in a story and making people heroes is so important. I knew I had to show the students they would be heroes of their story. That they were going to stand up and rise against the tide. I named the problem and then told them how we were going to solve it. You have to look directly at your actions and say how they will be fixed. As we met with the school leaders, we knew we needed a place for students to come. To be enriched in their lives, we would do that with the help of every mountain in the community. It started with them.

Finally, we went after the outcome. We knew that it had to be what students would look like if they came to the community center and how their lives would be changed by doing it. See, when it's all said and done, that 1 2 3 step approach makes the vision clear and concise. Didn't need anything else too crazy. Just Keep It Simple Superstar (KISS) We all love a good KISS!

Now you have your vision, you know how to articulate it. Now you need a crew. There are two levels to your crew. There are the heroes you will make and the guides that will get you there. Guides for you and the heroes. In the case of the community center, I had to share this vision with some adults who were willing to be hero makers with me. I had to find some men and women who wanted to make a change in kids' lives. I had to help them be the hero so they could make heroes. Get it? Donald Miller taught me in his Storybrand system that it is up to us to guide the story. I LOVE IT! Seriously, grab his book sometime and dig in. Hero on a Mission is fabulous if you want to get into community development.

Okay, I had my fanboy moment there. I did because it's so important to know that you will find people at different crew levels. Grabbing people who are more significant than you to pour into you as you pour out into others. It would help if you had those different levels. As you look at recruiting, you must identify where those people hang out and how to find the space to talk to them. Where are those spots they go to, and how do you get into the paths, like a good lion stalking its prey? You wait upon where they run so you can pounce! I mean recruit. Yes, recruit...

For me, it was local service organizations and churches. I spoke to those spaces and cast a vision. I went around and around and told the world about it. Then, as they told their friends, I started having people trickle in. This works every time. Every time I want to start something new, I go to the people in the mountains, cry out the vision, and see who wants to come along and travel the yellow brick road. Every story has it. Every great story has that band of characters: Wizard of Oz, Pirates of the Caribbean, Lord of the Rings. Harry Potter, blah blah, it's timeless! Know your audience and how the best way is for you to communicate as well. Do you write or speak better? Are you good with a crowd? You may have to find a writer because you say well. It may be finding someone to write as you don't articulate in words on paper well. Part of the recruitment is knowing who you need to help make your crew happen. Communication is a massive piece of it. There are face-to-face meetings, small and large groups, and someone you meet on the street. Are you ready to articulate that 3 step process in 30 seconds? Do you know how to talk about what you are doing so it catches someone to stop in their lives and want to engage it?

"I am tired of students not having hope. My community wants to build a place of refuge for students in the storm. So that when they spend time with us, they will be a hopeful, strong individual with a healthy self-identity."

BOOM! I know your mind is blown, and you hear that and want to join in... See, that is what I mean. Who wants to avoid helping in some way? Recruitment is a key to the success of what you do. Sharing that vision and letting it out there on Social media, Events like parades and festivals in your town. Get a booth and talk about it. I remember setting up at local events with a card table, a $30 banner from the local print shop, and business cards. I was telling anyone who would listen and getting email addresses. I wanted those addresses so I could speak into their world. I even asked for phone numbers. Phone numbers are even better as a way to communicate deeply with someone.

Gather your crew. Spend those times looking and casting that vision. You see, it's that vision that will get everyone ready to sail. Sail to the parts unknown. The waters that will create stories that rival the ages. It is time to plan that voyage and lead them to the gold!

7

STRATEGIC PLAYBOOK: CHESS MOVES FOR PROBLEM-SOLVING NINJAS

How do I rake? I am sorry, what? How do I use a rake? I was in shock. But I wasn't. Time and time again at the community center, I kept meeting students getting ready to head off into the real world, not knowing how to do some of the "work" related tasks in life. Using tools, operating equipment, and understanding how to talk to other humans around the work. Finally, just having the ability to engage and handle the workforce. It was so familiar. This gentleman, we will call Jimmy, couldn't grasp what that meant. For two years, I engaged with a program from the County that empowered students to work. Jimmy was my project. I had to teach him how to work in the next 10 weeks so that he would be productive in the workforce. HAH! If I grabbed Jimmy and started working with him, he would pick it up. That morning, I knew Jimmy was more than just someone to train. He was going to be a project. I thought I would have him be my shadow, and off we would go. Nope. I needed a plan. I needed a way to measure he was getting it and had to create a Show process. Do. Feedback. See that 3 steps. I needed to Show a student how to work. Let them Do it. Then, give the feedback for improvement. Little did I know I created a method that has assisted hundreds of students on the property over the past 8 years. I knew that I needed to have a plan to get things done. A plan that I could communicate to others who were also guiding and make it practical for everyone to get on board with. I had 3 other adults that worked with me. We all had the same mindset. Show. Do. Feedback. It worked, and it worked every time. We had a plan and worked with it.

Making plans can be an effortless thing. All great writers - I learned this from Donald Miller, too - start with the end of their story. What is it that they are trying to accomplish? See, if you know your ending, you can write the story..or, for us, the plan to get there. Working backwards. Even in this book, I worked backward. I knew who I was writing this for, but how would I get them to this spot of running their community development plan and executing it?

So you gather those strategic thinkers in your crew and sit before a whiteboard; a computer can work to about whiteboards are great for erasing and re-drawing and letting people have creative freedom. In the process, you will write on the board what the end goal is. Let's say that is step 10, which would be 9, then 8, then 7, then 6, then 5, 4, 3, 2, 1. You get it. Map it out. Look at what it will take to understand what you need to do.

Next, look at those steps and recognize the resources you will need to accomplish those steps. Is there someone you need to talk to? Do you need funds? Do you have to acquire some other kinds of resources? Mapping each step to resources is very important. Knowing what you need and when can also help when finding people in the mountains to help you along the way. Finally, take your crew and divide out the work. Who have you recruited, and what can they do? When we were renovating the building, one of the steps in the plan was to build a counter. I knew I needed some skilled people for some of it and other parts; I just needed some bodies to help me make it. With each step, we put who and what we needed. I needed wood. I needed screws, a saw, a tape measure, and 3 others to make it happen. one person to work with me to hold stuff and 2 people to measure and cut the pieces. We drew a plan of the counter, I communicated the pieces, and boom, we had a counter. 4 of us and our equipment and materials and a plan, and we got it done. Each step in your plan may have mini steps. That is okay. You keep working on the plan and the plans inside the plan.

Can you believe it? You have taken a frustration and learned how to make a vision. You have learned who in your communities and spheres can help you. You found a way to recruit people and understand that. Now it's time to talk about actually setting sail. When you set off and hit your first storm, what will it look like?

8

OBSTACLE OVERDRIVE: CRUSHING ROADBLOCKS LIKE A BOSS

I REMEMBER VIVIDLY LOOKING up at the ceiling and wondering how I would paint it. First, I am not a painter; second, I didn't know any painters; third, it was a 22-foot high ceiling. I remember laying on the hardwood floors looking up at the ceiling with 3 other students, our heads together in the corner like a flower looking up.

"How are we gonna get up there?"

"Can't we get one of those lifts in?"

"The ramp doors won't give us clearance, and the front steps are too brutal to try and carry one up."

"How about a ladder?"

"Could work for the edges, but that is too high for the center to move around with?"

"What about those scaffolds that they have on the sides of buildings?"

"Hmmm, didn't think about that?"

In a week, we had 4 stories worth of scaffolding to borrow. Just that simple. We had what we needed and were able to get it done efficiently. I broadcasted the need on social media and boom, we had it. WOW! After a bit of brainstorming, we got it done.

So often, when we hit hurdles, we stop. We stop in our tracks and don't move anymore. We look at the wall or ceiling and say we can't get over it. In reality, we need to run through experiments to find the proper results. In the case of the ceiling, it needed painting. I brainstormed and ran simulators in our minds, ladder, lift, etc. until we hit a solution that made sense. We often do not have the means to solve something, but we must think without a box.

The most significant phrase I learned is I know what I know, and I don't know what I don't know. That has always given me the freedom to be ignorant. I am not saying I stay ignorant, but ignorance and knowing it helps you understand the box you need to eliminate. So many times, we hear about thinking outside the box. I started living a life without a box and more about experiments. I look at things as experiments that I want to try out. I want to see if they will work.

Experiments are not failures or successes. Experiments give results; from those results, you can learn and eliminate your ignorance. I remember opening up a hangout for young adults and high school students. I had this excellent church facility that would allow for a video game arcade area, board game room, pool table, eating, and live music. It was awesome! I called it the Six Degrees Cafe, and it was glorious. People would come from miles around to hang out, and we had about 70 to 100 people each weekend chilling out and having fun. Then, as the weeks continued, a middle school or two students would appear. Then their elementary school siblings would come, and next thing you know, we are running a weekend babysitting service free of charge! Who would have guessed? It turned from a young adult hangout into a young student's place. Never saw that coming. Never saw it in a million years. Yet, those results showed us where and what was needed in our community then.

See, I could have said it was a failure, or instead, we created a killer babysitting time for parents, hah! Many times over and over, we need to see that failure is not an option. We must succeed at what we are doing. We are starting an experiment to achieve the results we are looking for. We want to keep working at things and keep trying stuff till we get the right ingredients. A good chef doesn't need a recipe, but they need the ingredients that can make something happen.

When you hit a hurdle, analyze it and run it through a simulator. Take data that you know from other projects. Call people doing something similar to you and ask for advice. As you hit hurdles and storms, you need to get creative. I want to leave you with one crazy hurdle to understand how to overcome.

It was COVID.

When COVID lockdowns happened in my state, it sent the world around me into a tizzy. A tizzy is an understatement. It was chaotic. There was nothing we could do to have any frame of reference. The only goal was to sail through the storm. Sail through versus weather because getting through it meant there was movement. I remember those days vividly because I started a new job as a pastor in a church. I was only there for 2 weeks before lockdowns happened, and the creativity had to flow. The goal was to keep a community together despite their regular practices to be a community. But we couldn't meet face to face. A community that was based on weekly or more gatherings that built unity through their shared beliefs. A community that thrived on face-to-face interactions is now relegated to being online. Do you remember it? So many different feelings and thoughts were brewing, and nobody had an honest answer they were sure of. EVERY-THING was an experiment. It didn't matter what we thought of; there was no guarantee of an outcome. We had to sail through it. We had to look forward, keep moving, keep trying, and read back the results. Constantly looking and finding ways to keep people relating and engaging. Weekly newsletters in the email, phone calls to their homes, and gatherings online in various ways. We got creative, and we stayed together.

The funny thing is most of those practices that got us through COVID have stuck. We have continued a lot of what we did then now. Some things fell off and were for that time only. Also, there were plenty of tries that could have been better results. In the end, we kept sailing through the storm. Sailing is not an efficient way to travel when it comes to distance traveled. The shortest distance between two points is a straight line. The fact is, when you sail, you only go in a straight line sometimes. You move the boat and the sails to keep you moving towards your destination. Sometimes fast, sometimes slow, and sometimes in between fast and slow. You feel the wind, and you work with it. Look over the horizon, plotting your course, and keep moving forward. When a storm hits as you sail, you use your charts and plans to guide you as you work through it. So often, reasonable plans are lost in the storms. When the storm hits, we often lose focus and do not keep moving forward and sailing. In the end, as you hit hurdles and hard times, keep flowing. Keep moving towards your goal, and you will get there. It may take years or days. You never know when the storm will break, and you come out on the other side doing so well.

Journeys aren't about how efficiently you do them. It's about the story that got you to the end! How you got there is such a testimony to your cause. Handling the hurdles and moving forward are the keys to success. Not stopping and still moving keeps us getting to our end goal. We only know we are getting to our end goal by getting feedback. I am learning to read how the wind is blowing, whether the crew is sailing well, and whether we are headed toward the rocks or open water. In the end, understanding where you are going and how you are getting there makes your story even more remarkable.

9

HARMONY IN VOICES: CRAFTING
FEEDBACK BEATS

THE GUITAR LET OUT a distorted chord, and the bass kicked in. Drums beating, you felt the tribal blues feel of the song. Lights whirled around the auditorium with a crowd of 5,000 teens and adults excited for the upcoming speaker. The lights buzzed around, and the music was pumping. The announcer made some intro like a WWE announcer, and boom, I stood up. Wearing a full-on steampunk outfit, I strutted down the stage in a larger-than-life fashion. Steampunk geared out tophat with a cane to boot. I was dressed to own the moment. Strutting down the aisle, I made my way to the stage, strutted around with the lights going, and then BOOM! I let out a mic-dropping address and was off to the races. Telling tales of my life and inspiring the students and their leaders to be more in their lives.

The overall presentation was a simple oration that I had set up. The tension for me was whether or not the crowd would participate. I wanted to make a standing wave from one corner to the next. It was something that I wasn't used to doing in such a large crowd. When you are speaking, crowd participation can be a hit or miss. I asked the gentleman in the front to stand on my mark, and everyone stood in a wave fashion... 1, 2, 3... he stood, and then the wave happened.

Watching 5,000 people stand as a representation of what one life can do to affect 5000. It was amazing to see it happen. Seat after seat, row after row of individuals taking a stand because the first person decided to. WOW!

Honestly, I had no idea if anybody cared about what I spoke about. You do not know if it worked when you let out a message of hope to people. Lights do not buzz in from people's seats to tell you if you did it. I don't have judges in the back giving me critique if I was effective. There are no built-in feedback systems. The only way I know if I made a difference is if I walk into the crowd at that moment and look for it.

So.... I changed around and walked out from the backstage area to the primary setting of the convention hall. People were bustling back and forth and moving about, heading to their next activity. We are at a week-long youth convention. Plenty of people were flowing and moving. I stood in the crowd, wondering if someone would say something to me.

A story I told was about surviving a drunk driving accident. I told you about this earlier regarding my friend Craig and how his mom, Elaine, stands up against drunk driving. I told the story from a perspective of pain and suffering and overcoming great odds.

She came up and looked at me. A young woman around 16-18 years of age. She looked at me and asked if she could hug me. I looked past her momentarily, and the youth group and leaders she was with were all standing around her in a supportive fashion. I reached out to receive her hug. She clutched onto me so tight I am unsure I have felt a hug that tight before. You could feel her breath as it quickened, and tears followed.

"Finally, I get to meet someone else and get a hug."

I held her, and she wept. I started to cry, but I'm not sure why. I just did. As we released our embraces, she wiped the tears from her eyes, looking at me. She began to tell me her car accident survivor story. She lost a friend she was driving with and felt so alone, with nobody else knowing how she felt. She had never met someone who could sympathize and understand what she felt. When I spoke, she knew I understood her. We talked more, and then the rest of her group engaged me, and we began to discuss what I had shared and engaged more and more on the topic. It was evident that what I had said mattered. My hope of inspiring someone to be a hero in their space worked. I knew what I did mattered.

Looking for ways to have feedback is essential in moving forward. We live in a culture prone to having feedback channels set up everywhere. I cannot go shopping with someone asking me for a customer survey. I love to read Google reviews of places I will eat for the first time. Feedback feedback feedback is how any good business or organization runs. Looking for the praise and the criticisms is how we can do a better job and know that we are making the mark. Feedback also doesn't just come from the end user but from those in your crew and the rest of your constituency. Feedback is essential. I want to look at 3 super quick ways of building in feedback to hear and engage with those you are working with and affecting.

Meetings, online systems, and peer feedback loops are the three main ways. These three simple feedback areas create a constant pulse to see if you are making the mark and sailing on course. Meetings are simple. Get people that are working with you together and meet up. It could be at a local coffee shop or on your back porch. Meetings are putting people in a room and catching up. I run feedback and planning meetings together. Always open up about how people are doing. If it is a regular meeting, I may ask for the highs and lows of their week. This allows people to open up and be heard beyond their work. Letting people talk about themselves humanizes the team. If we are always about getting down to business, we will need a more relational aspect that builds a good crew. Once we have that time, it is super easy to ask the question. "How are we doing?" Taking a moment to remind everyone why we exist and what the vision is, we can dig into answering the question. It is a great time to hear from your crew and assess the results and stories being told. In these meetings, note the positive and negative results that are happening. You can also set goals between now and the next time you meet. This allows you to keep track of your progress and show how you are moving toward where you want to be. It is a step-by-step process. One moment at a time, moving ahead. How have we done since last time? What do we need to change or tweak for the next time? What else do we want to get done by next time? How are we doing overall?

Simple meetings can take about an hour to two hours, depending on how many people and how chatty you can be. Setting the tone and keeping a pulse face-to-face is crucial. If your team is scattered, still get on that video call, see faces, and connect. Don't just rely on text or phone calls to get things done. Have the face-to-face and engage each other beyond the work. As a leader, lead through relationships. (Yes, probably another book in that.)

Relationships are crucial to the work we do as community developers. As you saw earlier, everything is related to our communities. Moment by moment, someone is affecting our space. Our world has developed a virtual way of connecting through social media. Social media is a power beast that can tear you to shreds or carry you across vast spaces. Social media truly is a tool to be wielded and understood. When I say understood, it is about who you want to communicate with. Getting your material out to those spaces creates a way of hearing back about what you are doing and whether it affects those who need to be impacted. Posting pictures and asking questions is a great way to see if you are hitting the mark. Engaging with online entities and asking questions to them. Find people, ask them to join your cause online, and listen to what they say. Often, it is in those interactions and soliciting feedback that you can see if you are making an impact. A quick story for you in this. The nonprofit bicycle shop I run is called Bike and Sol. I remember sitting around one day and typing this illustrious post on Facebook. It was a long rant about how we must equip the next generation to work well. I ran my mouth for probably 2 paragraphs and got onto a soap box. I posted it. It felt like a post that would be viral instantly! Nope. I had 3 likes, and barely anyone read it.

Recently, I snapped a picture of a student working. I wrote, "Training the next generation to work well. Who taught you to work well and how?" BOOM! We got instant feedback on it. Folks were posting and engaging. The approach was soliciting feedback. Asking questions and looking for answers. I didn't need to tell people stuff. I wanted them to hear. Social media can put you in touch with so many people so fast; it's such a gift and is a great tool. Learn it and engage it. Do a little surfing, and you can find great tools to get you started, or subscribe to a system that can work well for you. Listen to some podcasts, or look me up. I would be glad to help.

The third way of getting feedback is directly from your peers. Having those one-on-one sit-downs with your closest peers and finding out how things are going from their perspective. Back to our bike shop. I invite specific volunteers to breakfast on Saturday mornings. Typically, about 3 or 4 of us get together and engage on the deeper topics of the organization. Well, it's sometimes deep; sometimes, it's just what paint colors are the best. We continue to talk, mull, and figure out how we are sailing and if we are still hitting the mark. It is a constant engagement. I also ask how I am doing as the captain. Listening and engaging on how it is that we can do something better. Time and time, these peer-to-peer engagements yield high results in feedback and planning. Getting your closest crew members out for food and beverages and engaging on the more challenging topics. Listen to each other and build up from there. It will help in times of fast winds or stormy waters. Receiving the feedback also allows you to build a plan.

Feedback can sometimes generate a need for a plan. Creating a plan based on the feedback is a great way to engage and know that you are moving on the issues. Plans are simple. It is a way to start jotting down and making sure that you are moving forward month to month and getting what everyone agreed to get done. I like working on weekly, monthly, quarterly, and yearly time marks. Looking at ways that we can move forward in those time blocks. Moment by moment, putting down and plotting where we are going and what we are doing. Taking the feedback and showing the progress. It is a simple method. Just plot down what needs to be done each week, month, quarter, and year. Set the timeline out on a standing document and keep it in review. On a weekly and monthly basis, you can keep communicating where you are going and what is getting done. In the end, you show your progress, and you can measure your results.

This also comes in handy when sending reports or updating the public; you can map and show your results. I learned a long time ago if I keep good records, I can show how awesome my projects are. People love to hear a success story. If you are plotting and making progress week after week, you can also show what is happening. Remember, ask for feedback, engage the feedback, and report on the results. You will continuously progress and plot the course to accomplish the vision. You got this! Let's get into how we measure our success!

10

SUCCESS METRICS: BEYOND NUMBERS, IMPACT UNLEASHED

THE BEAUTIFUL VIEW at night above the Upper Perk Valley was stunning. Looking out over the night sky was a moment to behold. The clash of stars and street lights depicted what it is like to live in a rural, suburban setting. I took a moment to pause and reflect on this New Year's Eve. I was still determining what to expect. I invited many people to a not-so-open but open community center. I was there wondering if all this work was worth it for the long haul. Was I chasing a dream that would be a flash in the pan? The whole thing was a wonderment to me. I remember all the emotions of opening up after a few months of renovating and doing work. I knew it wasn't a pretty space but a space where people could gather. I set the ball in place and climbed down the ladders of the bell tower of the old church and knew that midnight would come soon enough, and we would drop the ball.

People showed up! Person after person came into the building. The high ceilings lit up with chandeliers and a beautiful Christmas tree. The space still needed paint and other amenities, but we were open for a party. Families and friends gathered around the circle tables, played games, and chatted. The night rolled on, some karaoke was sung, and laughter was heard. The fact is this. We did it. A rag-tag bunch of volunteers had created a community space within our community. Then, at midnight, as the clock struck, we lowered a yoga ball wrapped in Christmas lights from the bell tower to have our ball drop. YES! It was so. Dreams turned into reality. The long walk down the yellow brick road happened. Here we are from blueprints to reality.

See, the measure of success is simple. Did you do it? It's not matter how well, but did you do it? We often try to grade ourselves, but when you forge paths and try new things, the key is to ensure you go after the mark. What do you consider success?

Success comes in various ways when it comes to solving community problems. There are the successes along the trail and the immense success of getting where you are trying to get to. Recognizing that there are milestones along the way to keep you moving. Dorothy kept meandering down the road because she kept having success. Pulling in people along the way. Gathering her crew and having adventures. Overcoming the witch and heading to the Emerald City. So often, we get caught up in the main thing and need to remember the milestones.

Take time and think about the milestones you want to accomplish. What are the things that would make you feel successful and know you are on course? Is it buy-in from key leaders of your community? Have certain skill sets on your crew? Is it having a specific event happen? Raising a particular amount of money? What is it that you feel makes you successful and hits the marks? Time and time again, we focus so much on making sure our plans are correct, and we know about the end story, but what does it look like to monitor where you are at? Then you celebrate!

Celebrating wins is vital to keeping your crew motivated and sharing with the world that you are moving forward. So often, we get a task or a milestone and move on to the next thing. I would love for humanity to slow down sometimes and celebrate more! Think about birthdays. Birthdays are monumental in my family. We love to celebrate another year of a person's life. Why? Because each year marks another milestone in their life and our relationship with them. We also have milestones in humanity. For us, it can be 5 when we go to kindergarten, 13 when we become a teenager, and 16 when we can drive. 18 when you become an adult, and so forth and so on. As we continue to grow in life, we keep having milestones. Schooling, work, sports, and so forth, there is a lot of space for milestones and celebrations.

As I write this lately, I must celebrate more in some of my spaces. I observe in some more than others. Note to self. Celebrate the wins more! Celebrating doesn't have to be anything more than grabbing some ice cream or coffee from the local coffee shop. Whatever it is that your crew enjoys together, please do it!

As you hit the milestones, you want to be broadcasting that out. Shoot it out to the world that you are making a difference! As you communicate what you are doing, it will then, in turn, help others to get on board with your vision. As a leader, it shows the world you are leading! Leading is a journey, not just dropping anchor and keeping space. You are moving towards the end. As Dorothy moved along if she wasn't showing progress getting closer to OZ, then would the Tin Man keep going?

Remember, bragging about your team and its projects is okay. I need to improve in this area and work hard to brag about the accomplishments in my spaces. It's hard. Especially when it's your work. So often, we can point to others and praise them, but you need to be your biggest cheerleader. Standing up and telling the world what the workaround you are doing and that you are in the middle of it.

Finally, we have some wins and milestones behind us, and we are standing before the gates of the Emerald City. You are here. You have traveled the journey and are on the way to making those differences. How does it feel? Note to yourself and journal as you do. In time, you will be moving along and handling things. Now, I want to warn you. There is something important in all this work. You will keep doing this forever! HAH! When you hit something, you will be like I am frustrated,...and poof. You will talk about it with others. Find new people, build them up, and send them out to get it done. You, my friend, are an architect building solutions and will be excellent at it.

After affecting 19 organizations in the past 15 years, it is all about gathering people on the journey and empowering them to make a difference with you. I can hardly believe that it has become a lifestyle for me. So often, we step out into the world and see how awful it is. In the end, it's not. It is a garden lush with beauty that some caring and tending to will make it unforgettable.

So, go, take those frustrations and make a vision. Grab some folks to start walking with you. Head down that road, and may you find Oz.

www.ingramcontent.com/pod-product-compliance
Lightning Source LLC
Chambersburg PA
CBHW020133180726
47992CB00022B/2801